SABAH COLOUR GUIDE
KOTA KINABALU
& ENVIRONS

SABAH COLOUR GUIDE

KOTA KINABALU & ENVIRONS

WENDY HUTTON

Opus Publications
Kota Kinabalu
2009

Published by:

Opus Publications Sdn. Bhd. (183100-X)

A913, 9th Floor, Wisma Merdeka Phase 1,

P.O. Box 15566,

88864 Kota Kinabalu, Sabah, Malaysia.

Tel: 088-233098 Fax:088-240768

email: info@nhpborneo.com

Website: www.nhpborneo.com

Sabah Colour Guide: Kota Kinabalu & Environs

by Wendy Hutton

Design & layout by Hin-ching Chan

ISBN 978-983-3987-33-7

First published September 2009

Cover photo by Lee Yen Phin

Back cover by CV Chong

Printed in Malaysia.

CONTENTS

INTRODUCTION

Superbly located on a sheltered bay facing a scattering of exquisite tropical islands and coral reefs, and backed by the dramatic mountains of the Crocker Range, Kota Kinabalu has transformed itself from a simple trading post a century ago to an increasingly modern city, proud of its role as capital of the state of Sabah.

Sabah spreads across the northern tip of the world's third largest island, Borneo, with Kota Kinabalu strategically located roughly half-way along the west coast. Within one or two hours' drive of the city, an incredible range of places, activities and people await discovery. And standing sentinel over it all is the massive bulk of Mount Kinabalu, one of the highest mountains in Southeast Asia.

Simple fishing villages perch over the water not far from magnificent 5-star coastal resorts, while fertile paddy fields and clear mountain streams contrast with swamp forests where proboscis monkeys, crocodiles and fireflies can be seen. You can ride into the past on an old steam train; experience the thrills of white-water rafting, bird-watch in a reserve just a couple of kilometres from the centre of the city, paddle a sea kayak, go scuba diving or laze on powder-white sandy beaches. Or you could visit an orchid nursery or a sanctuary where young orangutan are taught to adapt to the wild, explore a native market and feast on fresh seafood in a city restaurant or at the side of a river.

This guide focuses on the city of Kota Kinabalu as well as major areas of interest along the west coast, from Kota Belud in the north down to the Klias Peninsula in the south. It also includes nearby islands, from Mantanani down to Pulau Tiga, as well as the islands of the Tunku Abdul Rahman Park, just off Kota Kinabalu.

© Sabah Museum

THE PHOENIX ARISES

*From fiery beginnings
to the rainforest city*

During the 18th and 19th centuries, when expansionist Europeans anxious for profit turned their eyes on Southeast Asia, the island of Borneo seemed a promising prize. There were several abortive settlements on the northernmost part of the huge island, but it was not until the sultans of both Brunei and Sulu signed an agreement in 1878 with an Austrian, Baron von Overbeck, that foreign powers gained real control of Sabah.

Von Overbeck sold his rights to the English Dent brothers, who created the British North Borneo Chartered Company which was subsequently given British government approval to run Sabah, renamed British North Borneo. The first capital was established in Kudat in 1882, but was moved to Sandakan (where a Resident had been put in charge of the east coast as early as 1879) a couple of years later.

In late 1882, the Chartered Company decided to establish a trading post on the west coast and chose Pulau Gaya. Gaya was already home to a scattering of Bajau fishermen (the name of the island comes from the Bajau word *goyoh*, meaning "big").

The small settlement of Jesselton, as Kota Kinabalu was then known, in 1911.

THE PHOENIX ARISES

The main street of Jesselton is today's Gaya Street, in what is known as KK Lama or "Old Kota Kinabalu".

The new settlement attracted a few Chinese shopkeepers as well as a short-lived sago factory. A visitor to Gaya just nine months after its establishment as a trading post declared that "for its admirable harbour and for other reasons, Gaya is likely to prove the most important post on the west coast of the Company's territory".

However, the intrusion of the British into northern Borneo did not go unchallenged. In 1897, a Bajau rebel, Mat Salleh, burned the Gaya settlement to the ground, forcing the Chartered Company to look for an alternative site. By mid-1899, a location on the mainland opposite had been identified: 30 acres of flat land adjacent to the coast where good anchorage was available.

By the end of the year, clearing of the land had begun, work was commenced on a breakwater and pier, and housing and government buildings were under construction. It was decided to name this new settlement Jesselton, in honour of one of the directors of the Chartered Company, Sir Charles Jessel.

The land selected for Jesselton was known to the locals as Api Api, the name of a type of mangrove tree (*Avicennia* spp.) which grew abundantly in the region, and which attracted thousands of twinkling fireflies at night. (The name Api Api has endured as the name of a political constituency in the city.)

The construction of a railway was begun far to the south of Jesselton in the 1890s, linking Beaufort and Weston, on Brunei Bay. However, when it was found that the bay was too shallow for deep-draught ships, a railway line was built from Beaufort north to Jesselton's port at Tanjung Lipat, boosting the importance of the settlement.

To help develop the land around Jesselton, the Chartered Company entered into an agreement with the Christian Basel Mission (which had already brought settlers into Kudat) to obtain Hakka agriculturalists. In 1913, three different batches of Hakkas were brought into Inanam, Menggatal and Telipok, small villages which already had a few indigenous settlements.

This region, north of today's city of Kota Kinabalu, became an agricultural hub, especially of small-scale rubber plantations. As time went on, other Chinese agriculturalists and traders established themselves along the west coast, with rubber estates (the larger ones controlled mostly by British planters) stretching southwards as far as Beaufort, and north around Tuaran district and Tenghilan, towards Kota Belud.

The Chinese were not the only group brought in to help develop North Borneo; a large number of Javanese were hired as labourers on the rubber plantations, and Sikhs employed as policemen. Many of these new arrivals remained to make their home in Sabah, their descendants contributing to the varied ethnic mix of Kota Kinabalu today.

The early days of Jesselton were peaceful and relatively uneventful. The few British residents soon established a sports ground and first played cricket on what is today's Padang Merdeka in 1901. By 1915, the Jesselton Sports Club was established, but since membership was restricted to Europeans, an Asian sporting club known as the Jesselton Recreation Club was opened soon afterwards.

Jesselton grew along the narrow strip of flat land between a ridge (Signal Hill) and the sea, but as the flat land was gradually built up, the process of reclamation — which continued well into the 1990s — was begun. Many locals solved the problem of land shortage by building houses on wooden stilts right over the shallow waters on the reefs. Today, only vestiges of the water villages or *kampung air* still stand, the majority having made way for refilling and the construction of commercial buildings and resorts.

Jesselton, like the rest of Sabah, was occupied by Japanese forces during WWII, and was the site of a courageous but abortive uprising in 1943. Allied forces eventually liberated Sabah, but bombing to dislodge the Japanese caused enormous destruction to the town. Sandakan, however, was almost totally obliterated and it was decided to move the capital across to less-damaged Jesselton in 1946. The Chartered Company could not afford the cost of post-war reconstruction, so they handed North Borneo to the British government to become a Crown Colony in 1946.

THE PHOENIX ARISES

In 1963, British North Borneo and neighbouring Sarawak decided to join the states of the Malay Peninsula and Singapore in the formation of the Federation of Malaysia (Singapore left the Federation two years later). North Borneo reverted to its original name of Sabah, and in 1967, changed the name of its capital from Jesselton to Kota Kinabalu (frequently abbreviated to KK).

The town continued to grow, with the post-war shophouses and utilitarian shopping districts slowly joined by more attractively designed modern buildings during the 1980s and 1990s. Highways were constructed and many new hotels and resorts built. As the population grew to around 300,000, Kota Kinabalu achieved city status in February 2000.

A programme of improving the city centre and planting trees and flowering shrubs has done much to enhance the appearance of Kota Kinabalu. The regeneration of certain downtown districts is continuing, and Sabahans look forward confidently to the day they can be even more proud of what has been dubbed The Rainforest City.

Because of a shortage of flat land, many houses were built on stilts over the shallow sea and reefs. Remnants of these water villages or *kampung air* can still be seen in parts of Kota Kinabalu.

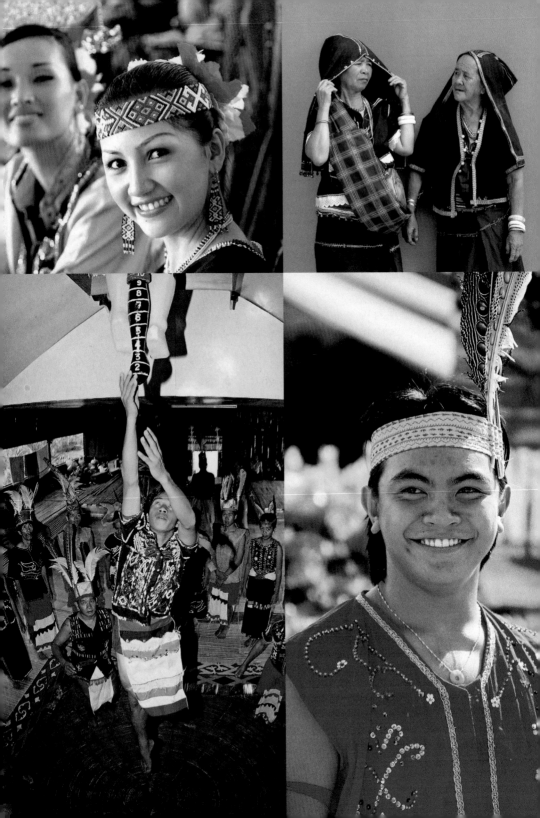

THE KADAZANDUSUN

The original inhabitants

As the capital of Sabah, Kota Kinabalu has grown into a diverse and multi-cultural city where most of the state's ethnic groups are represented. Specialists do not always agree just how many groups make up the complex ethnic picture of Sabah, although the figure of 35 is often mentioned. To simplify matters (albeit only slightly), Sabah's indigenous people speak languages which fall into four major linguistic families: the Dusunic, Paitanic, Murutic and Tidong.

The original people living on the west coast around today's city of Kota Kinabalu are part of the Dusunic language family. To the north and south of the city live sub-groups of this language family, such as the Lotud in Tuaran; the Dusun Tindal, Dusun Tabilung and Dusun Tempasuk in the Kota Belud region; the Dusun Tangara of Papar and the Dusun Tatana on the Klias Peninsula. The Dusun were joined in time by other groups including the Bajau, Irranun, Bisaya, Bruneian and Kedayan.

The Kadazandusun, the largest indigenous ethnic group in Sabah, includes many sub-groups, all with their own distinctive language and colourful costumes.

The Penampang district to the east of Kota Kinabalu is regarded as the Kadazandusun heartland. It was here, in the late 1950s, that the indigenous

Young Kadazandusun women vie for the title of Unduk Ngadau during the annual Harvest Festival celebrations each May.

people — through their leader Donald (later Tun Fuad) Stephens — claimed that all native Borneons speaking a Dusunic language were one entity and should therefore be given just one name: Kadazan. More recently, this term was changed to the more inclusive Kadazandusun.

The cultivation of rice in irrigated paddy fields was the cornerstone of west coast Kadazandusun life. Each stage of rice cultivation was bound up in ritual observances, culminating in a ceremony to give thanks for a successful harvest and to safeguard the rice spirit until the next planting. Ceremonies associated with rice growing (as well as healing and communicating with the spirits of the departed) are conducted by ritual priestesses known as *bobohizan*, who spent many years learning lengthy chants, all transmitted orally. The *bobohizan* are

literally a dying breed, and with increasing numbers of Kadazandusun following Christianity, together with the modernisation of Sabah societies, their services are seldom called upon and their age-old knowledge seems doomed to disappear.

Today, although many Kadazandusun still cultivate rice and other crops, they can be found in all walks of life in and around Kota Kinabalu. Many still don their traditional dress for special events, especially the Harvest Festival or Tadau Ka'amatan. The month-long Harvest Festival celebrations take place each May and provide an excellent opportunity to view many aspects of Kadazandusun culture.

There are demonstrations of handicrafts, traditional music, dancing and performances by ritual specialists, plus the chance to sample traditional foods and rice wine (*tapai* and *lihing*). Traditional contests and games are held, with the State-level celebrations culminating on 30th and 31st May, with special cultural shows, and the selection of the Unduk Ngadau or Beauty Queen.

EXPLORING KOTA KINABALU

The three most important factors for the success of a business are often given as location, location and location. The same is true for Kota Kinabalu, which owes its beginnings to the good fortune of a safe, sheltered harbour and a strip of flat land between the hills and the sea.

Its enviable location gives Kota Kinabalu a feeling of being on permanent holiday. While the city traffic, shops and markets are full of activity, there always seems to be patch of sea or an island in sight, a golf course or luxurious resort just nearby, a lushly wooded hill in the background or a long sandy beach to stroll along while watching a fabulous sunset.

The best place for an overview of Kota Kinabalu is the Signal Hill Observatory, reached by passing the Padang or town green. The small grassy **Padang Merdeka** has seen many a sporting match and parade during its century-old history, as well as being the site of the historic ceremony marking the formation of Malaysia in 1963.

The **Signal Hill Observatory**, located on the hills forming a lush green backdrop to the city, looks down over the ever-growing buildings and across the sea towards Pulau Gaya. Depending upon the time of day and the sunlight, the varying colours of the water and

Shutters are drawn across the front of old-style shophouses in the older parts of Kota Kinabalu at the end of each trading day.

Panoramic views over the city and Gaya Bay can be enjoyed from the Signal Hill Observatory (above). Every Sunday morning, Gaya Street is transformed into an open-air market, attracting locals and visitors alike.

reefs can be breathtaking, ranging from pale jade through deep turquoise.

The original centre of the Kota Kinabalu is aptly known today as KK Lama or Old KK, consisting of a few city blocks with **Jalan Gaya** as the epicentre. Beginning life as Bond Street, this was the heart of old Jesselton, the place to shop, go to the bank, visit a lawyer or frequent the coffee shop of the town's first modern hotel, The Jesselton, opened in 1954. Attractively restored in the late 1990s, this charming boutique hotel captures the ambience of that bygone era.

A block of shophouses along Jalan Gaya was the first part of the town to be rebuilt after WWII. Today, there is an intriguing mixture of businesses on the ground floor of the buildings along Jalan Gaya, the few remaining old Chinese provision shops and traditional medicine stores joined by modern appliance dealers, gift shops, coffee shops and restaurants. It's well worth a slow stroll down the street, stopping for a cool drink or perhaps a bowl of spicy noodle soup (*laksa*) in one of the open-fronted eating shops known locally as coffee shops or *kedai kopi*.

Every Sunday morning, from 8 am until noon, Jalan Gaya takes on the lively atmosphere of a local *tamu* or weekly market as four blocks of the road (from The Jesselton down to the end near the City Hall) are transformed for the **Gaya Street Fair**. Stalls lining both sides and the centre of the street offer a head-spinning range of produce — everything from orchids to puppies, antique coins to fruit trees, aquarium fish to woven baskets, handbags to souvenirs — to tempt shoppers and others who just go to soak up the atmosphere.

One of only two pre-war structures still remaining in KK, the two-storeyed white building in Jalan Gaya now housing the **Sabah Tourism Board** was built in 1916 as the government printing office. In 1936, it became the town's post office and remained as such until 1986. After total renovation, the gazetted historical building became the home of Sabah Tourism. Today, a ground-floor information centre offers advice and assistance to visitors.

The city's only other remaining pre-war relic is the **Atkinson Clock Tower**, on the lower slopes of Signal Hill facing the end of Jalan Jati. This delightful little white-painted wooden tower, holding a clock with just two faces, was built in 1905 to honour the memory of Jesselton's first district officer, Francis George Atkinson, who died of "Borneo fever" at the early age of 28. Incredible as it may seem today, with the clock all but obscured by high-rise buildings, the tower was once used as a navigational aid for shipping coming into the port.

An increasing number of outdoor restaurants and entertainment spots, especially on the bay at **The Waterfront** complex, are transforming parts of the city into a really pleasant place to meet, eat and relax, especially in the evenings.

While Jalan Gaya and Jalan Pantai remain the original business centre of the city, commercial life is concentrated in a few high-rise modern shopping complexes and older shopping districts. At one end of the town is the popular **Wisma Merdeka**, a multi-storey shopping and office complex in Jalan Tun Abdul Razak. The older shopping district of Segama (between the Hyatt and the General

Post Office) has a good mixture of inexpensive shops.

At the other end of the city, near The Waterfront, an attractive new shopping centre, **Warisan Square**, has a wide range of shops, including international fashion brands and food

The Atkinson Clock Tower (opposite, left) is one of only two structures to have survived WWII. A giant swordfish rises above the traffic roundabout near the Segama Waterfront (opposite, right). Downtown Kota Kinabalu (above) still has many older buildings.

chains. Nearby, the older but still popular **Centrepoint** offers a huge selection of shops (plus a more upmarket shopping floor known as Palm Square).

The open-air **Night Market** or Pasar Malam is held in Kampung Air (in the road near the High Court) every evening; cheap clothing, shoes, music cassettes, watches, local handicrafts and souvenirs are all on sale. After a bout of early evening shopping, visitors might be tempted to stroll a little further into Kampung Air to the restaurants of **Sri Selera Kampung Air**. This is officially open from 7 am–2 am, but really gets going around 5 pm every day, with a range of restaurants and food stalls under a high canopy offering a wide choice of food, everything from seafood to satay and Chinese pan-fried dumplings.

Much of this seafood has come via the fish market located next to **Central Market**, on the bay not far from the Segama complex and opposite KK Plaza. The Central Market is a fascinating place to explore. Mounds of local and imported fruit, glistening piles of vegetables, fragrant herbs and spices, sacks of rice, meat and dried produce are found on the ground floor, with cooked food stalls, inexpensive clothing and shoes upstairs.

The fish market — especially in the early morning — bears witness to the rich variety of marine life in the region with prawns, live crabs and other shellfish, pearly white squid and all kinds of fish from tiny silver anchovies to giant tuna and ray.

Not far from the Central Market, the **Handicraft Market** (locally known as the Filipino Market) is a warren of narrow alleyways crammed with handicrafts. Carved wooden spoons, baskets, mats, batik fabric and ceramics fill the aisles, with decorative shell lampshades or curtains and colourful mobiles dangling overhead. Although most of the goods come from the Philippines, there are some local Sabahan handicrafts as well as items from neighbouring Sarawak and Indonesia. This is an ideal place to browse for gifts and souvenirs, and bargaining is all part of the fun.

The ferry terminal for boats to the islands of Tunku Abdul Rahman Park, as well as the ferry to Labuan, has been constructed at **Jesselton Point**, beside the small protected basin of the Marine Police.

Fishing boats arrive with their catch (top left). Despite being one of Malaysia's fastest growing cities, Kota Kinabalu has a relaxed air (opposite, right top and bottom), although the pace picks up during Chinese New Year (opposite, right centre). the Handicraft Market (opposite, bottom left) is a favourite place to shop for souvenirs.

TOWARDS TANJUNG ARU

Inaugurated in 1965, the **Sabah State Museum** opened at its current hilltop location (about 5 minutes from downtown Kota Kinabalu) in 1984. The main building, architecturally inspired by a longhouse, contains the impressive Ceramics exhibit as well as galleries devoted to Archaeology, History, Ethnography and Natural History.

Two of the most interesting features in the Ethnography collection, on the lower level, are devoted to the uses of bamboo and to the colourful costumes and jewellery of eight of Sabah's ethnic groups. Also of interest to visitors, the "Tunnel of Time" is a largely photographic display of Sabah's history from the days of the British North Borneo Chartered Company in 1881.

The museum also maintains an ethno-botanical garden with a number of local medicinal and food plants, but for many visitors, the highlight is the museum's Heritage Village. This consists of authentic life-sized recreations of traditional homes, including Rungus and Murut longhouses which are located on a hill slope leading down to the small lake. Dotted about the lake, several other houses such as Bajau, Irranun and Bruneian can be explored, some of these containing a number of cooking utensils and everyday items which help bring them to life.

The typical early Chinese farm house is complete with kitchen utensils, good-luck charms pasted on the walls and an old radio set playing a Chinese radio station.

The Islamic Civilisation Museum or **Muzium Tamadun Islam**, located on the same hilltop as the Sabah State Museum (although reached by a different road), was opened in early 2001. The aim of the museum is to portray the history of Islam and Islamic culture within Sabah as well as in other states of Malaysia, in the Malay-Indonesian world (Nusantara) and in the Middle East.

Not far from both museums, the **Sabah State Mosque** in Jalan Tunku Abdul Rahman is an attractive example of modern Islamic architecture, its restrained dove-grey colour highlighted with small golden domes, dominated by the major dome and slender minaret.

The Sabah State Mosque, in Sembulan (above), was the state's largest mosque until recently. Tanjung Aru Beach (opposite) is a favourite place for locals to relax and to enjoy a snack or meal at one of the many foodstalls or restaurants.

Beyond the Sembulan roundabout and next to the Indian Association building on Jalan Tunku Abdul Rahman, the quaint wooden **Sikh temple** or Gurdwara looks vaguely like an English church with its Gothic-shaped stained glass windows and small hexagonal tower topped by a silver dome. This place of worship was built in 1924 for the local Sikh community, some of them descendants of the police brought in by the Chartered Company in the 1880s to help keep order in North Borneo. Every Sunday, members of the roughly 600-strong community gather for worship, then enjoy a communal vegetarian meal cooked by women volunteers in vast pans in the kitchen.

Kota Kinabalu's most popular area for relaxation, **Tanjung Aru Beach** stretches from a small headland occupied by the luxurious Shangri-La's Tanjung Aru Resort down to the front of the airport. Several grassy areas popular for camping and picnics, with clusters of food stalls, the Prince Philip Park and the private Kinabalu Yacht Club and Kinabalu Golf Club all located on this long, sweeping stretch of sand. People flock to Tanjung Aru Beach to relax, fly kites, play ball, bathe in the sea, enjoy a snack or a drink, or gaze at the famous sunsets with the fiery sun sinking dramatically into the South China Sea, silhouetting the islands of the Tunku Abdul Rahman Park.

A complex including a seafood restaurant, an upmarket restaurant specialising in Western cuisine, a coffee shop and an informal bar with beachfront tables has been built at what is locally known as **First Beach**. Next to this is a complex of food stalls, while another cluster of food stalls beyond Prince Philip Park, at **Second Beach**, sells Muslim food only.

TOWARDS LIKAS

Beyond the port area of Tanjung Lipat lies the wide shallow Likas Bay, backed by a series of mountain ranges, with Mount Kinabalu often seen towering in the distance. The land stretching down to the bay was once a swampy wetland, traces of which still remain in the Kota Kinabalu Wetland Centre and Likas Lagoon. A highway skirts the edge of Likas Bay, leading past the City Mosque and a cluster of food stalls (Anjung Selera) to arrive near the Sabah Foundation building before continuing on past the campus of Universiti Malaysia Sabah and the State Secretariat, and on up north towards Karambunai, Pantai Dalit and Sulaman.

To help preserve a small part of the important coastal wetlands which once dominated the Likas Bay region, the 24-hectare **Kota Kinabalu Wetland Centre** was gazetted in 1996. In 1998, it was designated a State Cultural Heritage Site and opened to the public in 2000. (The sanctuary is reached by a clearly indicated road off Jalan Istiadat).

The mangrove forests near Likas Bay are protected in the Kota Kinabalu Wetland Centre. White egrets and kingfishers are commonly seen, with many migratory birds visiting during the northern hemisphere winter.

Following the boardwalks above the brackish waters through the mangroves, with vivid kingfishers, Pacific Reef Egrets and other birds providing a splash of colour, it is hard to believe that the centre of the city is a mere 2 kilometres away. The sanctuary is an important breeding ground for many resident birds, as well as for several migratory species that arrive from northern Asia during the winter months.

The impressive **City Mosque**, its four slender minarets topped by blue domes and its huge onion-shaped dome delicately patterned in blue and yellow, is inspired by the design of the Nabawi Mosque in Medina. Dominating Likas Bay and set in a lake, this large mosque was completed in 1997 and can accommodate up to 12,000 worshippers.

The huge City Mosque, the largest in the state, sits in a moat overlooking the shallow waters of Likas Bay (above). Dominating the bay, the circular tower of Menara Tun Mustapha is home to the Sabah Foundation or Yayasan Sabah (right).

At the far end of the bay, **Menara Tun Mustapha**, the 32-storey circular tower of the Sabah Foundation (Yayasan Sabah) — its mirrored walls reflecting the sea or surrounding land — is somewhat of an architectural rarity being one of only five buildings in the world constructed entirely without pillars. An elegant revolving restaurant on the 18th floor offers stunning views.

Beyond the Sabah Foundation, on the highway leading towards Sepangar Bay, Karambunai and across the Mengkabong River towards Pantai Dalit, Sulaman and Tuaran, lies the campus of the **Universiti Malaysia Sabah**. Probably the most beautiful and spacious university in all Malaysia, the campus includes a waterfall, an indoor aquarium, a large mosque and even a jetty on the bay.

TUNKU ABDUL RAHMAN PARK

Swimming in exquisitely clear waters over a coral reef, not far from a white sandy beach backed by forest which is home to monkeys, hornbills and other wildlife, it seems impossible that a capital city is a mere 15–20 minutes away by speedboat. The islands of the Tunku Abdul Rahman Park are a must for visitors to Kota Kinabalu, and a popular place for relaxation with residents too.

Five islands form this marine park, which was gazetted in 1974: the largest of all, Gaya (part of which falls outside the Park); the almost circular little island of Sapi at the western tip of Gaya; Mamutik, the closest island to Tanjung Aru; Manukan, the most developed in terms of recreational facilities and accommodation, and the furthest island, seldom-visited Sulug.

Pulau Gaya, located opposite downtown Kota Kinabalu, has a settlement of local fishing families at its eastern end, as well as the private Gayana Eco-Resort adjacent to the Park's northeast boundary. Also located outside the Park boundary are several large water villages, houses built on stilts over the shallow waters of coastline, most of which are home to people who fled to Sabah in the 1970s to escape political unrest and violence in the southern Philippines.

Police Beach on Pulau Gaya is one of many idyllic bays within the Tunku Abdul Rahman Park.

All kinds of water sports can be enjoyed around the islands of the Tunku Abdul Rahman Park, a short speedboat ride from the city.

Most of the island is hilly and covered with original lowland forest. Close to the coastline, Gaya's lowland forest includes a range of typical shore plants, including a type of pandanus bearing a pineapple-like fruit. There is also a patch of mangrove forest which can be explored via a boardwalk not far from the Sabah Park's Base Camp (reached via a jetty in Camp Bay) on the southwestern side of the island. Mud skippers, crabs, birds (especially kingfishers) abound in this region.

Another novel activity can be enjoyed near the jetty in Camp Bay. Called "Sea Walking", this method of exploring the underwater world without the need for special scuba training and equipment was introduced by Sabah Parks, in conjunction with a private company. Wearing a special underwater helmet and assisted by two helpers and a diver, the visitor descends a few metres to the sea floor and explores an underwater trail for around 50 metres.

There is a network of forest trails on Gaya Island, and it is possible to continue beyond the mangrove boardwalk through beautiful forest (where huge monitor lizards and macaques may be spotted) down to Padang Point, a small bay immediately opposite the jetty of nearby Pulau Sapi.

The deeply indented Bulijong Bay on the northwestern side of Gaya leads in to **Police Beach**, which seems to have the softest, whitest sand in the entire Park. A private development is currently under construction at Police Beach, but hopefully the public will still be able to visit this idyllic beach to swim, snorkel, picnic or explore the trail which leads up over the hills, either down to Camp Bay or on to the small lighthouse on a headland.

Pulau Sapi, the smallest island in the Park, is so close to the tip of Gaya that it is possible to swim across. Sapi looks like a picture postcard for a beautiful tropical island and is very popular with tour operators, who bring groups of visitors here to swim or relax on the beach under the shade of the casuarina trees before enjoying a barbecue lunch. Coral reefs around the southern side of the island are popular with snorkellers, and also used by some dive operators as a training site for scuba diving.

A well-maintained jetty, picnic facilities, the possibility of snorkelling and sports equipment for hire, changing and toilet facilities all enhance Sapi's appeal, although it is definitely not for visitors seeking total privacy. As with all the islands in the Park, Sapi has walking trails. It is wise to avoid the sometimes aggressive macaques that frequent the beach area; do not feed them as they can be a menace to visitors.

Speedboats to the Tunku Abdul Rahman Park islands leave from the Jesselton Point jetty at Tanjung Lipat, site of the first port.

It's possible to "get away from it all" and relax near the sea within sight of the city by staying in one of the chalets (managed by Sutera Sanctuary Lodges) on **Pulau Manukan**. Once the site of a pre-war stone quarry, and probably settled by a few Bajau fishing families prior to that, part of Manukan Island was developed in the late 1980s and early 1990s.

A number of attractive wooden chalets nestle among the trees on the slope above the main beach. There are a restaurant, swimming pool, tennis court, souvenir shop, diving centre, a conference room, barbecue pits and picnic tables, and a playing field. A walking trail leads around the island, following the coast on the southern side before climbing up along the ridge on the northern side; to walk the entire trail will take about 1 1/2 hours. Manukan, very popular with tour groups and individual visitors, is easily reached using boats departing from the Jesselton Point ferry terminal and from the Sutera Harbour marina.

The closest island to Shangri-La's Tanjung Aru Resort and Sutera Harbour, **Pulau Mamutik** (which covers just 4 hectares as opposed to Manukan's 20 hectares) has several picnic tables set under the trees, a small café run by Sabah

TUNKU ABDUL RAHMAN PARK

Parks, a curving white sandy beach with a gentle slope on one side with a patch of interesting coral appealing to snorkellers, and a more dramatic drop-off near the jetty. However, the increasing number of tour groups now visiting Mamutik means that it is no longer a deserted paradise.

To the south of Manukan and Mamutik, **Pulau Sulug** is a round rocky island with a lovely white sandy finger jabbing into the waters of the South China Sea. It is the least visited island in the Park, and currently without any facilities.

Sulug is ideal for lovers of secluded spots, with shady places for a relaxing picnic, safe swimming and, for scuba divers, some of the best diving in the entire Park on the reefs off the southeastern part of the island.

Most dive operators offer **scuba** training courses, with classroom sessions as well as open water dives in the Tunku Abdul Rahman Park. In addition, qualified divers can arrange to dive in the Park with operators based in Kota Kinabalu.

The lack of strong currents and the relatively shallow depths make Kota Kinabalu an ideal place to learn scuba diving.

KADAZANDUSUN HEARTLAND

Penampang district, to the east of Kota Kinabalu, is the heartland of the original inhabitants of this part of the west coast. Small villages surrounded by rice paddies were once reached only on foot or along the rivers meandering through this fertile region at the foot of the Crocker Range. Today, a mixture of light industry clusters along the main Penampang Road and near the township of Donggongon, but it doesn't take long to discover peaceful rural areas as soon as the main road is left behind.

Although most traffic uses the by-pass road to Penampang, it is also possible to reach travel via Jalan Kolam, passing Bukit Padang and eventually turning right at a junction that leads to Kg Kasigui.

Just beyond the hospital at Bukit Padang, a left turn in Jalan Khidmat will take you past the **Sri Pasupathinath Hindu temple**, about 100 metres from the junction. Rebuilt in 2002, the temple retains some traditional elements of southern Indian temple architecture in its tower, with figures of deities in niches and statues of reclining cows along the roof. However, there is an unusual element of restraint, with figures in soft grey rather than the usual vivid rainbow of colours.

Despite the march of housing across land once dominated by paddy fields, some older Kadazan still fish in isolated pools and canals.

Shopping at the *tamu* or weekly market is as much a chance to socialise and browse as it is to find daily needs.

Jalan Kolam passes by the clearly signposted **Taman Tun Fuad**, a popular recreation area. Joggers pound up the hill trails of the park shortly after dawn and at dusk, while in the evening, many people come to enjoy a snack at the stalls or to eat at a popular seafood restaurant, built over a small lake. Also located within the Park, the **Water World Theme Park** is an excellent place to have fun, with its huge swimming pool and a range of water slides suitable for the whole family.

Kota Kinabalu's most interesting market provides an excellent opportunity to mingle with the Kadazandusun of Penampang district. Held every Thursday and Friday morning, the **Donggongon** *tamu* or market is known to canny city housewives as a great place for really fresh local fruits and vegetables at competitive prices. For visitors, it provides a fascinating glimpse of indigenous people in a totally non-touristy setting. The market is held in the special *tamu* area adjacent to the regular daily market building and with its raised cement walkways, shaded by a roof of traditional ironwood (*belian*) shingles, it is cool, clean and easy to explore.

KADAZANDUSUN HEARTLAND

Every Thursday and Friday morning, the Donggongon market or *tamu* offers a glimpse of a more traditional lifestyle. Everything is on sale, from dried seahorses (below) used in medicine to traditional jackets, fabric and basketware.

Descendants of a famous headhunter maintain the Monsopiad Cultural Village, which offers an insight into the cultural traditions of the Kadazan.

Billed as a "living museum", the **Monsopiad Cultural Village** — located in a picturesque semi-rural setting in Penampang district — is devoted to the history and culture of the Kadazandusun. It is run by the descendants of a famous Kadazan warrior and headhunter, Monsopiad, who lived in this location three centuries ago and who took 42 heads during his lifetime.

The Cultural Village consists of a number of buildings made of traditional split bamboo and thatch, as well as a riverside cafe, a performance area, a suspension bridge across the Moyog River, an old-style boat with thatch roof for river cruises and a souvenir shop, all set in a lush tropical garden. Local dances and music are featured daily.

In the House of Skulls, the heads taken by Monsopiad are suspended from the rafters and still honoured with occasional ritual ceremonies conducted by shamans or ritual priestesses known as *bobohizan*. Several display cases contain antique items used in these ceremonies, as well as the stunning headdresses, clothing, beads, brass hip belts, antique jars and other items used during rituals.

EXPLORING SOUTH OF KOTA KINABALU

From Kinarut to the
Klias Peninsula & Padas River

The old Papar Road (Jalan Papar Lama) leads to the **Lok Kawi Wildlife Park**, in a lovely garden setting about 30 minutes south of Kota Kinabalu. More than 100 animals, including Sabah's iconic Orangutan and the Proboscis Monkey, the Malayan Sun Bear, Borneo Pygmy Elephant and other native species can be viewed here in spacious and attractive surroundings. There is also a Children's Zoo and a series of beautiful gardens which are part of the Botanical Information Centre.

The village of **Kinarut**, just 20 km from Kota Kinabalu, consists of a few old wooden shophouses built when the railway halt was established. Most traffic heading south bypasses the village these days, following the newer coastal route through Kinarut Laut at the edge of a shallow bay.

The main attractions along Kinarut Bay and near the coast further south are several small resorts and a couple of restaurants.

The Lok Kawi Wildlife Park is a great place to discover some of Sabah's unique wildlife, including the Bornean Pygmy Elephant (left), Sun Bear (top Left), highly endangered Sumatran Rhinoceros (top centre) and Prevost's Squirrel (top right).

Steam train buffs will be delighted by a journey on the North Borneo Rail, with colonial-style carriages pulled by a 1950s engine through the countryside south of Kota Kinabalu.

Kinarut is also the departure point for **Pulau Dinawan**, a small island about 10 minutes by speedboat from the coast. The island, which has a lovely lagoon-like bay at one end, is uninhabited except for the Borneo Dinawan Village Resort (very popular with Chinese and Taiwanese visitors), at the other end of the island.

The railway line from Tanjung Aru is currently being relaid. When it is completed, steam train buffs will once again be able take a nostalgia trip on the **North Borneo Railway**. Five beautifully restored colonial-style carriages pulled by a 1950s' British Vulcan steam engine are reminiscent of the trains which started serving the state more than a century ago. The North Borneo Railway departs from the Tanjung Aru Station for a 4-hour return trip, passing by quaint villages, threading through mangrove and *nipah* swamps, rubber estates and scenic rice paddies to the coastal town of Papar. In keeping with the colonial theme, a meal is served in special "tiffin carriers" or lunch boxes during the trip.

The main coastal road from Kinarut to Papar passes the site of a huge plantation house built around 1910 for the manager of the Kinarut rubber estate.

It is no exaggeration to say that the development of the west coast, between Beaufort and Jesselton, was largely due to the construction of the railway line. When the British North Borneo Chartered Company took control of Sabah and attempted to open up this rugged, densely forested land — where travel was by foot, on buffalo or horseback or by boat — they were faced with the challenge of transporting produce grown in the fertile interior to the coast for export.

The managing director of the Chartered Company, William Cowie, appointed Arthur J. West to build a railway line from Bakau on the Klias Peninsula, leading north to Beaufort, and south to a port which was named Weston (after West himself). The first steam train, aptly called "Progress", ran from Bakau to Beaufort, but when the line from Bakau to Weston was completed in 1890, the Company (and West in particular) must have been highly embarrassed to discover that the shallow waters of Brunei Bay prevented sizeable ships from entering the port.

It was therefore decided that the railway line should travel north to Jesselton, terminating at the deep-water port of Tanjung Lipat. This stretch of railroad between Beaufort and Jesselton was completed in 1902, and three years later, the rail linking

The railway line was once the only form of transport to the south, and was vital in bringing out the produce of the fertile interior valleys.

Beaufort with Tenom was in use. By 1906, the line from Tenom was extended far as Melalap Estate, and was vital in transporting the rubber produced here and at the huge Sapong rubber plantation in the interior.

In the early years of the 20th century, wherever the land proved suitable along the line between Beaufort and Kinarut, rubber estates were established. Other produce such as tobacco and timber also travelled by rail, as well as passengers who took the only means of transport available through mangrove swamps, forests of *nipah* palm and rubber plantations on their way to and from the main west coast settlement of Jesselton.

The early days of the railway were not without challenges with storms, landslides, fallen trees and the disappearance of vital equipment commonplace. Some shareholders of the British North Borneo Company felt there was insufficient traffic to support the railway, complaining that it was "a railway through dense forests with nothing but monkeys as passengers". Nonetheless, the railway has endured, recovering from the destruction of rolling stock, bridges and tunnels during WWII.

"
a railway through dense forests with nothing but monkeys as passengers
"

Disgruntled British North Borneo Company Shareholder

The original 180 km of railway line was reduced to 134 km in 1963, and faster diesel locomotives replaced steam engines in 1971. The railway lines were upgraded, then starting in 2006, the entire railway network replaced. With the increasing use of what is Borneo's only commercial railway by tourists, and with plans for extending the railway line to allow it to provide greater service to oil palm plantations and industry, it is hoped that Sabah's railway will flourish well into the future.

Oil palm, Sabah's most important crop, is grown in parts of the Klias Peninsula.

Although only the building site remains today, this has been gazetted by the Sabah Museum and is known as **Panorama Kinarut Mansion** for its attractive views.

Just past the Sg Kawang bridge and popular with locals heading south from Kota Kinabalu is a spacious pavilion offering Taiwanese and local cuisine, the **Taiwanese Seafood & Steak Restaurant**. (Their beef noodles and stewed pork leg are particularly good.)

Although slightly slower than the coastal road, the old inland road to Papar is a far more attractive route, winding through picturesque valleys dotted with Kadazandusun villages, orchards and Sabah's biggest plant nursery before crossing the Papar River and the wide plains where rice is still grown in irrigated paddy fields. Here, it is easy to understand why Papar is sometimes referred to as the "rice bowl of Sabah".

A flock of Pacific Swallows sits on shrubs growing in the wetlands around the village of Garama.

Papar is a bustling riverside town almost 50 km south of Kota Kinabalu, a pleasant mixture of older wooden Chinese shophouses and new developments, with plenty of flowering shrubs and trees near the town centre. Perhaps the most striking building in Papar is the Chinese temple, located slightly downriver of the town centre and approached by a beautifully planted driveway along the river, with even a few willows for a classical Chinese look.

The road to Beaufort continues past **Kimanis Bay**, its name derived from the word for cinnamon, *kayu manis*, obtained from the bark of trees which once grew in the region. (A road leading from Kimanis to Keningau passes Sabah Parks' Crocker Range Park headquarters, about 30 minutes' drive away.)

Boats cruise the canals and rivers each afternoon in search of wildlife (above), encountering local transport and a few houses en route (opposite).

The next major village south of Kimanis is **Bongawan**, which retains more of a flavour of the past than any other village along the west coast. Take a voyage back in time by turning right at the roundabout on the main Beaufort road, crossing the railway line and turning into the original village of Pekan Bongawan. The three blocks of 2-storey, pre-war wooden shophouses lining both sides of the short main street not far the old railway siding positively breathe nostalgia.

The **Klias Peninsula** juts into the South China Sea, separating Kimanis Bay from Brunei Bay. Built up over the eons by the flow of silt brought down by the Padas and other rivers, the peninsula was almost entirely covered by peat swamp forest rich in mangrove trees, *nipah*, *nibong* and sago palm until less than 50 years ago. Even today, the peninsula has the largest area of coastal wetlands along Sabah's west coast, and current studies may result in the gazetting of more areas for preservation in addition to the current Klias Forest Reserve.

Coastal wetland forests help stabilise the coastline, preventing erosion, and are an important breeding ground for fish. Used sustainably, they provide material for building, such as water-resistant *nibong* trunks for piles of houses or jetties built over the sea, *nipah* and sago palm fronds for thatch, and certain types of mangrove wood (*bakau*) for piling, scaffolding and charcoal.

The wetlands also provide a home for a variety of birds, especially egrets, the large orange-beaked Stork-billed Kingfisher and turquoise White-collared Kingfisher. It is also possible to spot Borneo's unique proboscis monkey, as well as macaques and, with lots of luck, silver leaf monkeys. Large congregations of fireflies can be seen in many of the mangrove trees at night, with fruit bats visiting the trees to pollinate their flowers.

The Klias Peninsula is home to an interesting mixture of peoples: Muslim Bisaya, Kedayan and Brunei, many of them living in fishing villages along the estuaries; the largely Christian Dusun Tatana, who incorporate some Chinese observances in their rituals, and a number of Chinese, some of whose ancestors came here almost a century ago.

Several species of pitcher plant grow abundantly in and around the Binsuluk Forest Reserve, including these clusters of *Nepenthes gracilis*.

Increasing interest in exploring the fascinating wetlands of the peninsula or in relaxing on the lovely beaches on the northwestern side mean that the Klias Peninsula is finally starting to attract visitors. Large tracts of swamp forest can still be found, especially near Weston, as well as a few patches around Binsuluk on the northern side of the peninsula.

There are two ways to reach **Kuala Penyu**, the district administrative centre located on an estuary on the northeast of Klias Peninsula. Although the Kuala Penyu road (leading off the main road about 7 km before Beaufort) is faster, a more scenic secondary route turns off the main road 72 km south of Kota Kinabalu. This road leads eventually to the vehicular ferry crossing the river at Kuala Penyu,

Small patches of forest still stand in the wetlands of the Klias Peninsula.

passing several attractive villages including Kg Brunei and Kg Pimping, before skirting the beaches along the southern end of Kimanis Bay and passing Kg Binsuluk.

The Binsuluk swamp forest (despite much of it having been destroyed by fire in recent years) has patches of several species of pitcher plants as well as magnificent *nibong* and *nipah* palms, and patches of typical mangrove trees known locally as *bakau*; a surprisingly good view of the vegetation can be enjoyed even from the road. The Binsuluk estuary is a good spot for bird watching (the Blue-throated Bee Eater is often spotted on the electricity lines), and the locals often come here to fish or catch crabs.

The sago palms once prolific on the Klias Peninsula provided an important source of food for the local people, who obtained sago paste (*ambuyat*) by grating the interior of the trunk of mature palms, rinsing the pith in water to get the starchy residue. Known here as *rumbia*, the sago palm is the star of the local Pesta Rumbia, held annually in July or August at Pantai Sawangan, a beach about 7 km from Kuala Penyu. Various local competitions and games are held, often including competitions such as weaving the fronds of sago palm to make thatch or racing water buffaloes.

EXPLORING SOUTH OF KOTA KINABALU

Pantai Sawangan, while a pleasant picnic area, is by no means the most attractive beach. Further south, at Kg Tempurong (a particularly well-maintained small village), there are a couple of simple resorts, and public access to a long stretch of white sandy beach shaded by tall trees is easily obtained at the edge of the village.

The main road across the peninsula linking Beaufort with Kuala Penyu and Mempakul (where a ferry leaves for Labuan) crosses the **Klias River** at the village of Kota Klias. An increasing number of tour operators offer a late-afternoon/early evening river cruise along the Klias River through wetland forest to watch out for proboscis monkeys, macaques and fireflies, following it with an early dinner before the 2-hour drive back to Kota Kinabalu.

Apart from the lodges near the Klias River, several can be found around **Kampung Garama** on the western side of the peninsula. The newest and arguably most attractive of these (run by Only in Borneo Sdn Bhd, sister company of the white-water rafting specialist, Riverbug) has attractive accommodation for overnight visitors, although the majority return to Kota Kinabalu after dinner.

Living Lighthouses

Fishermen living around mangrove areas have observed for generations that certain types of firefly make their home in *Sonneratia* mangrove trees. Their tiny blinking lights can be seen from a reasonable distance, and fishermen returning on dark nights have been known to use the twinkling fireflies as a navigational aid, knowing that the trees in which the fireflies cluster mark the edge of the waterway.

Set over swampy land beside a canal which leads to the Garama River, the well-designed and efficiently run Garama River Lodge has almost one kilometre of wooden boardwalks. Small boats leave the canal just metres from the lodge at around 4 pm for a cruise through the mangrove forests, passing an atmospheric and almost deserted village accessible only by river and eventually linking up with the Klias River.

It is generally possible to get surprisingly good views of the remarkable proboscis monkey, a primate found only in Borneo, in the forests along the river. With its huge pendulous nose and pot belly, long white tail and grey and orange fur, the male proboscis is indeed a most splendid creature. As the day cools down, small groups of young male

Proboscis monkeys congregrate in trees at the riverside in the late afternoon, making them easy to see.

proboscis play-fight, mothers gaze tenderly at their infants, and dominant males rule the roost as they munch on their last few leaves of the day.

If you're lucky, you'll see the setting sun before heading back for your lodge, passing huge congregations of water buffaloes enjoying a final bath before settling for the night. Flocks of white herons perch in the trees like Christmas decorations, while thousands of fireflies flicker on and off like Christmas lights — truly a wonderful spectacle.

The lucky visitor who stays overnight will enjoy the peace and beauty of the countryside around Garama River Lodge, the star-studded sky (weather permitting) rivalling the fireflies close by. And in the early morning, a stroll down the long boardwalk to the river keeps visitors well above the swampy ground and enables them to look at the plants, birds and butterflies.

Another interesting area of the Klias Peninsula is near **Weston**, about 120 km from Kota Kinabalu. Reached by a sealed road off the Beaufort–Sipitang road, Weston is a village that never achieved the grand vision of the Chartered

Company. Planned as a major port for shipping out produce brought by rail from the interior, the shallow seas approaching Weston made it impossible for shipping to tie up at the jetty, so it was eventually bypassed in favour of Tanjung Lipat, Jesselton's deep-water port.

An ideal base for exploration of the wetlands, and also for discovering pitcher plants and other interesting species in the dry lowland forest behind, **Weston Wetland Paradise** is located less than 5 minutes by speedboat from the village. A wooden lodge perched over the edge of the estuary provides the ideal vantage

Water buffaloes are a common sight in lowland rice fields and in parts of the Klias Peninsula.

point for watching fireflies twinkling in the nearby trees at night, and for observing the huge fruit bats flapping by, as well as for enjoying a feast of freshly caught crabs, relaxing or watching local fishing boats heading for the sea.

Boat trips help visitors discover the beauty and variety of the mangrove forests, which are far from the stereotyped image of densely packed, monotonous trees in an unpleasant muddy swamp. Channels cutting through a *nipah* palm forest and threading back into the Padas river penetrate a whole different world, nothing but *nipah* palms as far as the eye can see (which, to be honest, isn't very far in such a densely packed environment).

These beautiful palms have bulbous black stem bases plunging into the water, stems which were once dried, burned and sifted to obtain salt. The lush green fronds of the *nipah* are dried to make thatch for roofing, and the palm ribs can be used to make walls. The dusty orange spathes and flowers also have their uses, with sap from the inflorescence of *nipah* palms boiled to make palm sugar. The edible fruit, contained inside large brown pods, is like a firm transparent jelly, and a popular addition to a mixture of fruits, cooked sweet beans and shaved ice.

Other areas of the Weston wetlands show the strategies used by certain trees to survive in this water-logged, salty environment. Some, such as the *Rhizphora apiculata*, have branching stilt roots, part of the roots standing high above the water and allowing the tree to breathe. Others, like the *Sonneratia caseolaris* and *Avicennia* spp., have peg-like roots projecting up from the mud, performing the same function. Fringing areas of the wetlands can be surprisingly beautiful, with the fragrant white flowers of the Mangrove Trumpet Tree floating on the water, or clusters of long white and pink stamens of the *Sonneratia* flower dangling overhead.

The young shoots of the *Sonneratia* (one of several varieties of mangrove tree) are the favourite food of the proboscis monkey, although sightings of these animals near Weston are far fewer than along the Garama and Klias rivers.

Behind the riverside lodge of Weston Wetland Paradise, a high boardwalk leads to the accommodation which is built on dry land, and from here, trails lead into a 10-hectare forest filled with pitcher plants, thorny rattan vines, sea hibiscus and a variety of other plants. The *Nepenthes gracilis* forms thick carpets of tiny pitchers along the ground in some areas, or twines its way up over other plants. The fat little jugs of the *Nepenthes ampullaria* can also be easily seen, while there are also sites dominated by *Nepenthes rafflesiana*.

When the American participants of the first TV Survivor series, filmed on **Pulau Tiga**, were debating the political correctness of eating rats, little did they realise that a resort restaurant was only an hour away. The producer made sure they never caught sight of Pulau Tiga Resort, which would have

The jetty at Pulau Tiga, often called Survivor Island after a TV reality series was filmed there.

destroyed their illusion of being on a deserted island in the South China Sea. (See Accommodation for information on Pulau Tiga Resort.)

Pulau Tiga, together with two nearby islands, is protected as a marine park and has Sabah Parks' staff accommodation and a small headquarters on the same bay as the resort. The island is just under 30 nautical miles from Kota Kinabalu, but

the easiest way to reach it is by speedboat (which takes around half an hour) from Kuala Penyu.

There are several easy jungle trails through the tall rainforest on Pulau Tiga, where macaques, squirrels and monitor lizards can often be seen, especially behind the Pulau Tiga Resort's kitchen! The birdlife includes the shy chicken-like megapode bird, which buries its eggs in the sand and lets the heat of the sun do the incubation — unless a monitor lizard helps itself to a tasty treat. The rare Nicobar pigeon used to be a migratory visitor on Pulau Tiga, but today, only the more common Grey Imperial Pigeon is seen. Confident black and white Magpie Robins, with their melodious call, are common in open areas.

Pulau Tiga offers a couple of curious mud volcanoes where fine, tepid grey mud burps as gases are gently released from the earth. A mud bath has been dug for those who want to wallow like water buffaloes and become covered with what some believe to be therapeutic mud.

North of Pulau Tiga, there is tiny wisp of blinding white sand, an "almost-island" bathed by water in every shade of blue and turquoise. Rocky Kalampunian Damit, also known as Snake Island, is off limits unless permission has been obtained from Sabah Parks because it is an important breeding ground for sea snakes.

The warm silty mud bubbling up from Pulau Tiga's mud volcanoes make them a popular spot for visitors (top). Monitor lizards abound on the island, especially around the resorts (above).

Beaufort is the main town in Sabah's southwest, 100 km and about one-and-a-half hours by road from Kota Kinabalu. It is somewhat surprising to learn that the road to Beaufort was completed only in the 1970s, and prior to that, the railway was the only way to travel south.

Trains began operating from Beaufort along the Padas Gorge to Tenom in 1905, and although the construction of a road has been discussed from time to time, the train service remains the only link to this day. Most passengers between Beaufort and Tenom use the slow, fan-cooled train; there is also a quaint little railcar holding 13 passengers which travels daily along the line, and can be specially booked for rafting tours.

The train through the Padas gorge pauses at Pangi, a small station 39 km along the river, which is the starting point for most rafting trips. After being briefed, visitors take to the inflatable rafts, which are safely guided by professional rafters, and begin a 9-km ride that reaches peak levels of excitement in rapids with evocative names such as Merry Go Round and Head Hunter. Although the virgin forest which once covered the nearby hills no longer exists, there are still many lovely wild areas which can be enjoyed during the quieter moments of the trip.

When the water level is high, some of the rapids can be classified as grade III (grade V is the maximum), promising a really exhilarating ride. The rafting finishes at Kg Rayoh, where appetites sharpened by the morning ride are satisfied with a barbecue lunch. Then it's time for the train back to Beaufort, followed by the road trip to Kota Kinabalu. All in all, a long but exciting day.

White-water rafting along the Padas River offers plenty of high-adrenalin excitement.

HEADING NORTH

Tuaran, the Kiulu Valley and on to Kota Belud

The main road leading north from the city, Jalan Tuaran, passes a couple of interesting Chinese temples. Located about 4 km from the city centre, the **Che Sui Khor Moral Uplifting Society** is housed in a spectacular traditional Chinese pavilion, all orange tiles and bright vermilion pillars, with an 11-storey pagoda topped with gleaming green tiles behind.

Just before the junction of the main highway north, a hillock on the left of Jalan Tuaran is dominated by the city's largest Chinese temple, the **Poh Toh Tse Buddhist Temple**. A staircase flanked by large statues of various deities leads to the entrance of the classically constructed temple (built in 1980), while a giant statue of the Goddess of Mercy dominates the grounds.

The striking main building and pagoda of the Che Sui Khor Moral Uplifting Society (opposite).

To reach the floral beauties of **Orchid De Villa**, take the old Jalan Tuaran through Inanam (avoiding the main highway north, the Jalan Tuaran Bypass). Turn right towards Pekan Inanam at the roundabout into Jalan Kionsom and travel for 2.5 km until just before the bridge over Sungei Kitobu, where a sign to the right indicates the way to this large commercial orchid centre in Kg Kawakaan.

Orchid De Villa is Kota Kinabalu's only large-scale commercial grower of orchids for the florist trade. These beautiful hybrid orchids are just one of the attractions in this lush, well-maintained garden. Of particular interest are the many native orchid species, festooned on tree trunks,

Colourful displays of hybrid orchids are joined by rare native orchids (above) at Orchid De Villa, on the outskirts of Kota Kinabalu.

spilling over cool streams or nestling on the ground in situations which duplicate their natural habitat.

Beautifully located in a cool, wooded valley just below the Kiansom Waterfall several kilometres beyond the turnoff to Orchid De Villa, **Mari-Mari Cultural Village** offers visitors the chance to experience the culture of five major ethnic groups found in western Sabah.

Traditional houses in thatch, bamboo and bark have been recreated, with each ethnic group sharing certain skills with the visitor. Learn to cook in a bamboo tube Dusun-style; discover how the Rungus make a fire from a tube of bamboo; help beat out bark to make cloth with the Lundayeh; prepare deep-fried cakes with the Bajau and try leaping on a springing platform in a Murut longhouse. After a cultural show with dances, a meal is enjoyed in an airy hill-top pavilion, with the sound of the nearby river (spanned by a traditional suspension bridge).

A scenic drive (recommended for 4-wheel drive vehicles) can be enjoyed by taking Jalan Kobuni (to the left just before the waterfall) up the hill to the tiny Dusun village of Bambangan, situated about 600 metres above sea level. A road runs along the ridge, eventually passing through **Kg Kokol** and coming down to

Potteries near Telipok offer many items with distinctive local motifs.

join the main road just north of Menggatal. Breathtaking views can be had on either side of the ridge, down over Sepangar Bay and south beyond Kota Kinabalu, and dramatic vistas over the forested mountains leading up to Mount Kinabalu.

The highway north of Inanam passes the village of **Telipok**, where the old farmhouses are rapidly being replaced by new housing estates and industrial developments. One thing that still remains is the **pottery industry** established by several Chinese families slightly north of Telipok. The largest of these, Ng Sian Hap, is located on the right of the road at Kg Bakut, 29 km from Kota Kinabalu. A huge selection of garden pots, lamp stands, decorative vases and large incised jars is on sale here, as well as a range of handicrafts aimed at the tourist trade. It is interesting to watch the creation of the pottery (except on Sundays), especially the incising of patterns and painting of the glazes, processes which take place immediately behind the main sales room.

There are two routes from Kota Kinabalu to the resort and recreation area of **Karambunai**. One is to go via Likas Bay and take the new highway past Universiti Malaysia Sabah, eventually turning left on to Sepangar Bay Road; the alternative is to take the old highway past Inanam and turn left at the clearly marked junction of Sepangar Bay Road. This leads to Sepangar Bay (site of a Malaysian Navy base), with a turnoff just before the bay to Karamabunai.

Karambunai Resort spreads over a peninsula wedged between a long beach washed by the South China Sea and a lagoon at one side of the mouth of the Mengkabong River. Star of this is the luxurious Nexus Karambunai Resort, next to an 18-hole golf course.

A highway off Sepangar Bay Road before Karambunai passes the Kota Kinabalu Industrial Park, a large new polytechnic college and an oil storage terminal then continues over a large bridge across the Mengkabong River. If the weather is clear, it is possible to get fine views of Mount Kinabalu.

Mengkabong was once the major centre for Sabah's west coast Bajau, renowned as fearless seafarers and skilled fishermen who traded in dried salted fish and salt, making this by

A rare quiet moment at Karambunai, where a popular resort is located between the sea and a golf course.

burning water-soaked *nipah* palms. The village, greatly reduced in size and importance today, is made up of houses perched on foundations over the shallow waters of the river, although the picturesque thatch houses of bygone days have disappeared.

North of the Mengkabong River, there has been a large amount of development in the past decade, with areas of swamp forest cleared, resorts built along the coast and a number of restaurants established. The "resorts" in the Tuaran district, from Karambunai all the way north to Surusup on the Sulaman River, range from luxurious, international properties including the luxurious **Shangri-La's Rasa Ria Resort** at Dalit Bay to very basic accommodation where the facilities are strictly limited. There are three golf courses in the Tuaran coastal region, at Karambunai, Dalit Bay and at the Mimpian Jadi Resort, and all major resorts in the area offer a range of sea sports. Fast roads with clearly marked signboards make it

The fishing village of Penambawan still has a number of traditional houses.

easy to visit this region, and it is possible to completely bypass Tuaran, following Jalan Sulaman all the way to **Kg Serusup**, a village on the edge of a large estuary on the Sulaman River. (When driving into the village, beware of the unmarked speed bumps and large amounts of animal manure on the road.) Serusup itself has no major attractions — apart from a very basic "resort" inspired by traditional Bajau architecture, with attap thatch covering the wooden walls and roof of the restaurant and chalets perched over the water.

Just 10 minutes by speedboat from Kg Serusup, **Penambawan** (perhaps the most traditional Bajau fishing village still in existence on Sabah's west coast) is reached only by water. The estuary here is so wide that it is known as Sulaman Lake, fringed by mangroves which provide building material such as water-resistant *nibong* palms, *nipah* thatch for walls and roofs and mangrove poles for beams. There are dozens of traditional houses in Kg Penambawan, where the main livelihood is still fishing.

The main boardwalks of the two jetties and the "highways" across the village — which is entirely built over the water — are made of sawn timber, but many of the boardwalks linking the densely packed houses consist of an assortment of poles and planks. The village is always full of activity and colour: women sort and salt fish for drying; cook over a wood fire, hang flowery sarongs to dry, paddle ashore in search of fresh water or chat to neighbours while soothing a baby suspended in a sarong cradle. Many of the men still go fishing in old-style dugout canoes made from a single log.

The fertile river plains around **Tuaran** supported the west coast's largest concentration of indigenous Kadazandusun, as well as Bajau and Irranun, long before Sabah was taken over by the British North Borneo Company. In the early years of the 20th century, Tuaran was a flourishing agricultural and trading centre where the Lotud (a sub-group of the Kadazandusun), as well as Dusun from inland near Tamparuli, Bajau from Mengkabong and Javanese from the nearby rubber estates rubbed shoulders with Chinese shopkeepers and artisans.

Today, linked to Kota Kinabalu by two highways, Tuaran is about 40 minutes away, and the surrounding paddy fields are increasingly giving way to housing estates and commercial developments. Resorts at Pantai Dalit and Sabandar Bay have increased the number of visitors coming to Tuaran district, and the small town centre is thriving, especially on Sunday, the day of the weekly market or *tamu*.

Tuaran's *tamu* sprawls over the lanes and open ground around the regular market building, right to the edge of the Tuaran River. There's almost sure to be a set of traditional gongs made by the Rungus from Kudat, the vendor demonstrating their almost hypnotic resonance — a counterpoint to the latest Canto-pop, Kadazandusun melodies or Malay love songs blasting out from the CD stalls.

As Tuaran is not far from the sea, it is renowned for its fresh seafood and many housewives from Kota Kinabalu travel to the *tamu* early on Sunday in search of bamboo clam shells, sailfish cutlets, gleaming squid and bunches of edible seaweed resembling miniature green grapes.

Cooler climate vegetables grown on the slopes of Mount Kinabalu are brought down to Tuaran by Kadazandusun women, who take home with them bundles of wild fern tips or heart of palm sold by the Tuaran Lotud. If you can't wait to get home to cook what you've just bought, there are plenty of stalls offering ready-cooked food, including leaf-wrapped savouries, deep-fried patties and sticky sweet cakes.

If the *tamu* food doesn't appeal, try Tuaran's famous Chinese-style fried noodles (*char mien* Tuaran) at Tai Fatt coffee shop on the main road, a couple of

A popular local version of Chinese-style fried noodles can be enjoyed at Tuaran.

doors up from the Orchid Hotel. Their delicious (albeit cholesterol and fat-laden) combination of fried fresh wheat noodles, three types of pork, egg and green vegetable is enough to keep you going as you explore the Tuaran district.

Still in Tuaran district, but reached by turning right at a roundabout before Tuaran town, the small town of **Tamparuli** is on the Kiulu River. This is the last spot of flat land before the main road starts its climb over the Crocker Range towards Mount Kinabalu and on to Sabah's east coast. The name of the town is immortalised in the popular local song, *Jambatan Tamparuli*, about its original suspension bridge. Today, a modern road bridge bypasses the town, although there is still a cement causeway across the river into Tamparuli on the old road; as this causeway is subject to flooding (giving rise to its local nickname, the "underwater bridge"), a high pedestrian-only suspension bridge has been constructed beside it.

The trading centre for the fertile Kadazandusun villages in the region, Tamparuli has a pleasant, old-fashioned feel. During the Wednesday market or *tamu*, the village is abuzz with social and commercial activity, with a wide range of vegetables and fruits from the mountains mingling with seafood brought in from Tuaran and clothing, household goods and farming equipment from the city on display.

One of the most scenic regions close to Kota Kinabalu is the lovely valley through which the **Kiulu River** flows, bubbling over rounded stones before it widens and slows at Tamparuli. Suspension bridges linking picturesque villages, terraced paddy fields with lumbering water buffaloes and their constant companions, the white egrets, and a river that promises a refreshing swim and a picnic in a shady spot are reasons enough to visit the Kiulu valley. However, there is even more to attract visitors, as the Kiulu region has become popular for outdoor adventure activities, especially white-water rafting and tubing.

Although the rafting here is not as demanding as it can be at its best along the Padas River above Beaufort, the surroundings are particularly scenic and the level

THE LOTUD

Lotud women playing gongs at a traditional ceremony.

Among the most striking traditional costumes seen in Sabah are those worn by the Lotud of Tuaran district. A subgroup of the Kadazandusun, the Lotud were known for their ritual priestesses or *tantagas*, who were skilled in rainmaking ceremonies and also in rituals to appease spirits believed to inhabit huge sacred ceramic jars or *gusi*. Owing to modernisation and the adoption of Christianity by most Lotud, traditional ceremonies are rarely held today.

Only the ritual specialists are permitted to wear a long-sleeved blouse (other woman wear short sleeves).

The striking head ornament worn by Lotud women consists of a headband made from strip of *nipah* leaf dyed red, inset with a band of beaten gold. Stuck into the bun of hair pulled to the back of the head, a further decoration made of four bundles of chicken feathers dyed bright red, plus a few black feathers and some dangling beads adds the finishing touch to the headgear. Further enhancing the impact of the traditional outfit, hip bands of thin rattan dyed bright red are slung over a black sarong with colourful insets of needle-stitch embroidery, with jewellery and a long scarf completing the outfit.

of excitement is ideal for beginners and families. Another advantage is that rafting trips begin at a point in the Kiulu River less than one-and-a-half hours from Kota Kinabalu, half the time that it takes to reach the Padas rafting departure sites.

Most tour operators can arrange rafting in the Kiulu, but the expert (and a tourism award winner for their adventure packages) and the only one to offer white-water kayaking as well as rafting is River Bug. The company maintains an Adventure Centre at Kg Rangalau (around 7 km along Jalan Tamparuli–Kiulu), set in a beautiful riverside location facing a steep forest-covered hill.

This centre is used as the finishing point for rafting trips. Happy rafters can indulge in the pleasure of showering in an enclosed garden-like bathroom, and relax in fan-cooled dining pavilions where an appetite built up by the morning's rafting can be satisfied with a barbecue lunch. The adventure centre is also used for either individuals or groups interested in trekking, jungle survival, camping and discovering the local lifestyle (ever fancied helping to plant or harvest rice?).

Continuing up the valley beyond the village of Kiulu, the road eventually comes to **Kg Pukak**, where a dirt road leading down the hill into a hairpin bend near the school eventually comes out on a flat grassy stretch at the river's edge. About 50 metres upriver from the suspension bridge is a delightful shady picnic spot, with deep pools on the far side of the river ideal for swimming.

Each year (normally in October but check with Sabah Tourism), the locals along the Kiulu River organise an unusual sporting fest known as the **Kiulu 4M Challenge**. The name comes from the Kadazandusun words for the traditional sporting activities involved: *manangkus* (running); *memangkar* (bamboo rafting); *manampatau* (swimming with a bamboo pole) and *mamarampanau* (stilt walking). The event, which is open to non-locals as well, is normally full of humour as well as excitement and a spirit of competition among the various categories participating.

One of the most beautiful districts along the west coast, **Kota Belud** spreads over the fertile Tempasuk plain to the west of Mount Kinabalu and south to include Ambong Bay. Attractive villages are shaded by fruit trees and splashed with vivid flowers; paddy fields glow emerald green or gold, depending on the stage of the rice cycle; water buffaloes wallow in swampy ground, almost always in the company of slender snowy white egrets. Sparkling clear rivers, formed by waters spilling from the steep slopes of Mount Kinabalu, cut their way across the Tempasuk plain, rushing over stones or boulders smoothed over thousands of years.

COWBOYS OF THE EAST

A Bajau farmer riding his water buffalo to go ploughing in the paddy fields of Kota Belud district.

There is a myth among Sabah's Bajau that they are descended from Malays of Johor, at the southern tip of the Malay Peninsula. When escorting a princess to marry the Sultan of Brunei, they were (the story goes) attacked at sea and the princess carried off. Fearful of returning to Johor and facing the wrath of the princess's father, they settled along the coast of Sabah. Anthropological and linguistic research, however, confirms that the Bajau came to Sabah from islands south of Mindanao (now part of the Philippines), where they are known as the Sama.

The first record of Bajau in the west of Sabah goes back to the 16th century. It seems that the earliest Bajau settlements were concentrated around Mengkabong and the Tempasuk plain of the Kota Belud district on the west coast of Sabah, while later related groups settled around the islands off Semporna on Sabah's east coast. Unlike their eastern counterparts, most of whom still make their livelihood from fishing, the majority of the west coast Bajau gave up their seafaring ways and adopted life on land with a vengeance. They became farmers, planting rice and raising cattle. And in the process, they became skilled horsemen, riding on small local ponies, earning themselves the nickname, Cowboys of the East.

On ceremonial occasions, the Bajau horsemen don their traditional dress with woven folded headgear, brilliant satin jackets enhanced by embroidery and loose trousers. Their ponies are perhaps even more gaily decorated, draped with embroidered cloth and often a type of head covering, with a saddle fixed on a special blanket and a necklace of bells strung about the ponies' necks. Nothing can match the striking arrival of a group of Bajau horsemen in ceremonial dress, something that happens on special state occasions and during the annual Tamu Besar held at Kota Belud.

The rivers spill out into estuaries or bays, with beaches ranging from the almost black sand beach north of Pulau Usukan, stretching on up to Rampayan Laut, to the softer creamy sand beaches south of Ambong Bay. Patches of mangrove swamp still cover some shallow coastal land, with a few fish ponds starting to encroach on these.

And always, Mount Kinabalu looms in the background, sometimes brooding and grey, at times playing a coy dance with veils of cloud. In the early hours of the morning, the mountain sometimes seems so close that you feel you could reach out and touch the cold purple-tinged pinnacles thrusting into the sky.

The original inhabitants, the Dusun, have worked the Kota Belud area as farmers for countless generations. Those living in the north of the Tempasuk plain, towards the Kudat district, are known as the Dusun Tabilung, while those around the Tempasuk river basin are the Dusun Tempasuk. The group living to the south, bordering Tuaran district, call themselves Dusun Tindal. Kota Belud region has, however, now become synonymous with the Bajau, many of whom moved here from Mengkabong a century or more ago.

The township of Kota Belud (the name means "Fort on the Hill") grew up near the site of the market or *tamu* which used to be held every 20 days, a custom that seems to have been in existence for at least two centuries. Known as the Tamu Darat (Land Market), it was held on neutral ground where the indigenous pagan Dusun could meet the Bajau, Irranun and Obian Muslims to trade. In 1906, the British North Borneo Company appointed a District Officer who was based in Kota Belud to oversee the district, which was much smaller and considered more lawless than Tuaran.

The town of Kota Belud has changed radically over the past couple of decades. All but one of the old blocks of wooden shophouses have disappeared (most destroyed by fire) and the old market in the centre of town — with its huge shady trees — has given way to a modern administrative and shopping complex with Islamic architectural overtones. Traditional Bajau houses are no longer seen in the villages of Kota Belud district, although the carved crossed poles at the apex of the main roof are still a feature of some homes. (For a look at a traditional Bajau home, visit the Heritage Village at Sabah Museum in Kota Kinabalu.)

For most visitors, Kota Belud is synonymous with the Sunday morning *tamu*, the biggest and the most varied weekly market in Sabah, which attracts sellers from as far as 150 km away. The fascinating mixture of people is matched by the profusion of goods on sale. Bajau women wearing the Muslim headscarf squat behind piles of fresh or dried seafood; elderly Kadazandusun women with a wad of chewing tobacco tucked firmly in one cheek peer out from under conical woven hats as they consider a string of pickled fish; wizened Rungus grannies dressed in homespun black sarongs wear a fortune in antique beads around their necks, yet sometimes go bare-footed; glib-talking Buginese medicine men draw crowds with their cure-everything potions; vendors from the city preside over stalls of hardware, kitchen goods, agricultural chemicals and racks of inexpensive clothing, while Irranun or Bajau men with long headscarves preen their colourful roosters. Occasionally there may be Murut medicine sellers peddling their potions, while Ranau tobacco merchants offer their home-grown produce.

The Sunday *tamu* is held at a special ground about 1 km from the centre of the town. The Tamu Besar, an annual festival celebrating Bajau culture, is held in Kota Belud during October or November. A special feature of this festival is the delicious traditional cakes, sweetmeats and savouries on sale, as well as displays of handicrafts and traditional music to entertain the crowds. Perhaps the most popular events of all are the buffalo races and dramatic displays given by the Bajau horsemen.

The old way of fashioning steel blades is still practised by Encik Bakar in an open workshop in the large garden of his Kg Siasai home, which fronts the sparkling wide Tempasuk River. His father and his grandfather before him made *parang*, and his two sons are already working with him. For a fee of RM5, visitors are welcome to watch the hand-operated bellows quickly heat a charcoal fire. Bakar selects a flat piece of steel (he generally recycles old car springs) and thrusts it into the glowing coals, leaving it until it is literally red hot. He then beats the steel and re-heats it, repeating the process countless times until the steel is shaped into a blade with a point at one end and a haft to fit into a wooden handle at the other. The blade is then sharpened with an electrical grinder (a break with tradition here), and one of his sons crafts a wooden scabbard or sheath for the *parang*.

At the first roundabout on the Kota Belud bypass, a road to the left leads to **Usukan Bay**, used as a port in the early days of British North Borneo for produce shipped in or out of the district of Kota Belud.

Road signs are sometimes missing, but if drivers keep to the road, ignoring all turns to the right they will eventually come to the high curving bridge spanning the Tempasuk River, with Pulau Usukan visible a few hundred metres away. **Kg Kuala Abai**, which spreads over both sides of the river is a popular place with amateur fishermen who cast their lines from the comfort of the Restoran Tanjung Keramat.

The road terminates about 1 km further on at a small Bajau village on Usukan Bay, used as a departure point for trips to **Pulau Mantanani**, a group of three islands about an hour away by speedboat.

Only the largest of the islands (Mantanani Besar) is settled, home to Obian fishing families, some of whose ancestors came from the southern Philippines at least a century ago. Further south lies uninhabited Mantanani Kecil where the simple wooden Mari Mari Dive Lodge perches on stilts over the sea. This island, together with a small rocky islet, Lingisan, close to the southern tip of the Mantanani Besar, is protected as a bird sanctuary.

Two types of birds are of particular interest at Mantanani: swiflets which make edible nests which are gathered from rocky hollows and small caves on the main island, and two species of tropical frigate birds. A dramatic spectacle can be seen each dusk around the main island of Mantanani as thousands of huge black frigate birds come in to roost in the trees on the slopes of rocky Lingisan, which make it possible for them to get airborne the next day.

The Mantanani islands offer some of the best scuba diving off Sabah's west coast. Some scuba divers visit on a day-trip, relaxing over lunch at the facilities maintained by Scuba Paradise on a beautiful sandy spit on the northeast of Mantanani Besar. Others who prefer to stay overnight do so at Mari-Mari Dive Lodge or Borneo Sea Adventures' resort on Mantanani Besar's southern bay. Like anywhere else, the visibility is variable, sometimes affected by plankton in January and February, and best from December to March during the northeast monsoon.

Around 20 dive sites have been identified on the relatively shallow coral reefs around Mantanani, where hard and soft corals, anemones, vividly coloured reef fish in all shapes and sizes, and a large number of nudibranchs make each dive a voyage of non-stop discovery. And as if this weren't enough, there are also marine turtles, dolphins and sightings of the rare dugong or sea cow, a mammal which gave rise to the legend of the mermaid.

A small resort is poised over the sea at Mantanani Kecil.

SOUTH CHINA SEA

WATER FRONT
ESPLANADE | FILIPINO MARKET | CE M

PLAZA WAWASAN

OCEAN SEAFOOD VILLAGE

PROME NADE | MARINA COURT

WARISAN SQUARE

LE MÉRIDIEN

API API CENTRE

CENTRE POINT

SINSU

RAN

STAR CITY

STAR CI TY

ASIA CITY

SEDCO SQ.

KAM PUNG AIR

NIGHT MARKET

C
CH

POLICE STATION

ALL SAINTS CHURCH

CHUNG HWA LIKAS

WISMA BUDAYA

GSC CINEMA

CATHAY CIN EMA

BAN dar AN BERJAYA

LON DISTAN BUS TAXIS

k A R A MUN SING

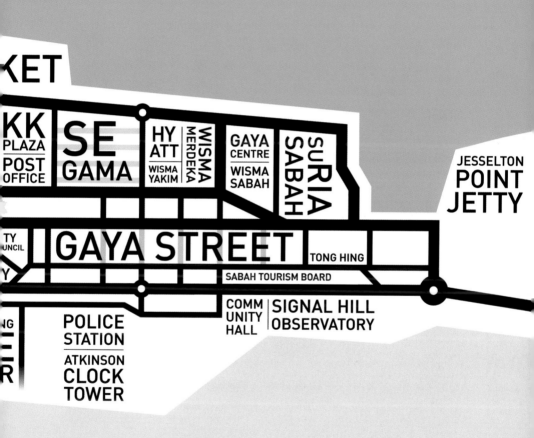

Sabah Tourism Board
51 Jalan Gaya
tel (088) 212121 / *fax* (088) 212075
info@sabahtourism.com
www.sabahtourism.com

Located in a restored building originally constructed in 1916, Sabah Tourism's information counter has helpful and friendly staff, and a rack of tourism brochures in several languages. Their constantly updated website is a helpful place to find a wide range of information, including festivals and special events. Open from 8 am–5 pm Monday to Friday, 9 am–4 pm Saturday to Sunday.

Sabah Parks
Block K, Lot 1–3
(next to Alliance Bank)
Jalan Tun Fuad Stephens
tel (088) 211881 / *fax* (088) 212719

The Sabah Parks administrative office is located in the Sinsuran shopping complex. Apply here for permission to camp on the islands of Tunku Abdul Rahman Park. All other accommodation within the various Parks (except for Crocker Range Park) is now managed by Sutera Sanctuary Lodges.

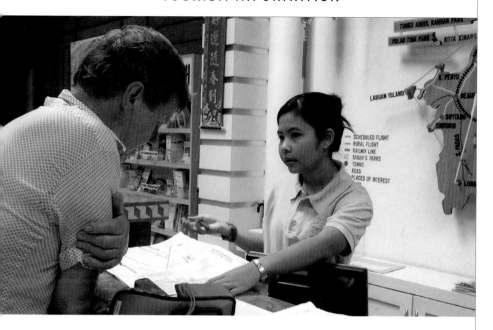

Sri Pelancongan Sabah
Ground floor, Block L,
Sinsuran Complex
tel (088) 232121 / *fax* (088) 265540
info@sabahtourism.com
www.sabahtourism.com

Located in the road parallel to (and directly behind) the office of Sabah Parks, this is a subsidiary of Sabah Tourism Board. Sri Pelancongan specialises in organising all kinds of tourism-related events, as well as offering free brochures on accommodation, tours, coming events etc, the monthly *Sabah Tourism Bulletin*; the helpful staff will answer any queries. There is also a gift shop with a range of locally-made handicrafts and souvenirs. Open 8 am–5 pm Monday to Friday, 8 am–4 pm Saturday.

Kindawan Riding Centre
Tuaran Beach Resort,
Syabandar Bay, Tuaran
tel (088) 793 593 / (016) 837 1855
ridingkindawan@yahoo.com
www.kindawan.com

Pleasure rides and riding lessons are
available, including relaxing rides along
Sabandar beach (RM120) and longer rides
through the surrounding countryside
and nearby village. Riding times: 6.30 am
–10.30 am; 3–6.30 pm.
Hotel transfers available.

KK Wetland Centre
off Jalan Bukit Bendera Upper, Likas
tel (088) 246 955
8 am–6 pm Tuesday–Sunday
RM10 (non-Malaysians)
RM3 (Malaysians)

Lok Kawi Wildlife Park
Old Papar Road
Open 9.30 am–4.30 pm daily.
RM20 (Non-Malaysians)
RM10 (Malaysians)
(RM5 children).

Mari Mari Cultural Village
Traverse Tours Sdn Bhd
Wisma Sabah, Lot 227–229, 2nd
Floor, Jalan Tun Fuad Stephens
tel (088) 260501 / (088) 260502
Hotline: (019) 8204921

Guided tours are by prior arrangement,
with tours at 10 am, 3 pm and 7 pm. Tariffs
range from RM130–RM150 and include
transfers, house tour and demos, cultural
show and buffet lunch, high tea or dinner.

Monsopiad Cultural Village
Kg Kua Kandazon, Penampang
tel (088) 774 337
mcv@monsopiad.org
www.monsopiad.com
9 am–5 pm daily
(cultural dances at 9.30 am,
11 am, 2 pm and 4 pm; guided
tours whenever required)
RM60 (non-Malaysians)
RM45 (Malaysians)

Muzium Tamadun Islam Sabah

Jalan Menteri, off Jalan
Tunku Abdul Rahman
tel (088) 538228
9 am–5 pm
RM15 (non-Malaysians)
RM2 (Malaysians)
students free

North Borneo Railway

Contact Sutera Harbour Resort
tel (088) 303 352

At the time of publication, service is
suspended while the railroad is relaid.
Contact the resort to check if the 4-hour
return trip to Papar has resumed.

Orchid De Villa

Km 6, Kg Kawakaan,
off Jalan Kiansom, Inanam
tel (088) 434 997
orchiddevilla@yahoo.com
8 am-5 pm Tuesday to Sunday
RM20 (non-Malaysians)
RM10 (Malaysians)
RM5 (children)
Inclusive of guided tour.

Sabah State Museum

Jalan Muzium, off Jalan Penampang
tel (088) 253 199
9 am–5 pm
RM15 (non-Malaysians)
RM2 (Malaysians)
students free

Tunku Abdul Rahman Park

For entry to Pulau Gaya, Pulau Sapi,
Pulau Mamutik and Pulau Manukan.
RM10 (non-Malaysians)
RM3 (Malaysians)

Scuba divers are required to pay
for a permit to dive within the Park
RM50 (Non-Malaysians)
RM20 (Malaysians) for a 1-day permit.
The dive operator will arrange
for payment.

TOUR OPERATORS

Borneo Divers & Sea Sports
9th floor Menara Jubili
53 Jalan Gaya
tel (088) 222 226 / *fax* (088) 221 550
information@borneodivers.info
www.borneodivers.info

This premier dive operator offers diving to Pulau Sipadan and Labuan, and maintains a base on the island of Mamutik within the Tunku Abdul Rahman Park, where they conduct a full range of PADI diving courses as well as operate pleasure dives.

Borneo Sea Walking Sdn Bhd
Suite S 1, 4th Floor, Wisma SEDCO,
Lorong Wawasan Plaza,
Coastal Highway, Sabah.
tel (088) 249 115 / *fax* (088) 249 116
franliew@tm.net.my

This company offers non-swimmers and those without any experience to see part of a coral reef off Pulau Gaya by donning a helmet with a breathing tube.

Riverbug/Only in Borneo Traverse Tours Sdn Bhd
2nd floor, Lot 228–229 Wisma Sabah
Jalan Tun Fuad Stephen
tel (088) 260 501 / *fax* (088) 261 503
riverbug@traversetours.com
www.traversetours.com

This award-winning operator arranges rafting trips in both Kiulu and Padas rivers, the Mari Mari Cultural Village and Mari Mari Dive Resort. They also operate a white-water kayaking school, while their sister company, Only in Borneo, operates the Garama River Lodge, ideal for viewing proboscis monkeys, fireflies, birds and other wildlife on the Klias Peninsula.

Diethelm Borneo Expeditions
3rd floor Bangunan Uni Asia
1 Jalan Sagunting, Kota Kinabalu
tel (088) 263353 / *fax* (088) 260353
dbex@tm.net.my

Tours to all major places of interest in Sabah are offered by this operator specialising in adventure tours, including white-water rafting and trekking. They are the only ones to maintain their own lodge on the Padas River.

Sabah Air
Sabah Air Building, Old Airport Road
tel (088) 484733 / *fax* (088) 484372
enquiry@sabahair.com.my
www.sabahair.com.my

For the ultimate view of Kota Kinabalu and the nearby islands, take a 20-minute helicopter sightseeing tour from the airport. RM260 per person.

Scuba Paradise
G28, Wisma Sabah, Jalan Tun Razak
tel (088) 266695 / *fax* (088) 236695
info@scubaparadiseborneo.com.my
www.scubaparadiseborneo.com.my

Specialising in day trips for divers and snorkellers to the island of Mantanani, this company also offers diving around Kota Kinabalu and Pulau Sipadan.

TYK Adventure Tours
Lot 48, 2nd floor, Beverly Hills Plaza,
Jalan Bundasan, Penampang
tel (088) 720826, 727825 / *fax* (088) 720827
tykadto@tm.net.my
www.tykadventuretours.com

An award-winning adventure tour specialist organising a wide range of trips, including mountain biking, trekking through the forest adjacent to Kinabalu Park and tours to the Weston wetlands.

A network of **mini-buses** serves areas within Kota Kinabalu as well as plying routes to towns along the west coast, from Beaufort in the south up to Kota Belud in the north. The mini-bus station is located opposite Wawasan Plaza shopping complex.

Large **buses** serve a number of suburban areas; buses to the beach of Tanjung Aru can be taken from the bus station between City Hall and the Post Office. Long-distance buses leave from near the Padang except those to the east coast which leave from the large bus interchange in Inanam.

Air-conditioned **taxis**, which can be hailed in the street and from taxi ranks around the city, are moderately priced. Taxis leaving from the airport must be paid for in advance at the taxi counter. Although most taxis in the city have meters, few drivers will use them so the fare must be negotiated in advance. Taxis can be hired on an hourly basis; contact Sabah Tourism for recommended drivers.

Boat services to the Tunku Abdul Rahman Park, as well as ferries to Labuan, leave from the Jesselton Point ferry terminal next to the Marine Police in Jalan Haji Saman. Boat operators charge from RM10–RM20 for a round trip to the marine park, depending on the island; a boat to Police Beach will cost around RM80. Boats also leave for Tunku Abdul Rahman Park from the marinas at Sutera Harbour Resort and Shangri-La's Tanjung Aru Resort.

This listing offers a very small cross section of the wide range of accommodation available in Kota Kinabalu and its environs. For a full listing, please check with Sabah Tourism Board or Sri Pelancongan Sabah.

EXPENSIVE

Hyatt Regency Kinabalu
Jalan Datuk Salleh Sulung
tel (088) 221234 / *fax* (088) 218909
bchrkk@tm.net.my
www.hyatt.com

The oldest five-star hotel in Kota Kinabalu, the pleasantly refurbished and redecorated Hyatt is located in the centre of the city, facing the bay. A wide range of amenities and services, with popular restaurants featuring Japanese and Chinese cuisine.

Shangri-La's Tanjung Aru Resort
tel (088) 225800 / *fax* (088) 244871
star@po.jaring.my
www.shangri-la.com

Sabah's first luxurious resort and part of a chain of resorts and hotels, this occupies a lushly planted headland at one end of Tanjung Aru beach. This spacious resort offers a wide range of sporting activities, with two swimming pools, gym, tennis courts, bicycles, table tennis, a marina and a range of restaurants and bars.

Sutera Harbour Resort
tel (088) 312222 / *fax* (088) 317540
reservations@suterah.com.my
www.suterharbour.com

Built on 384 acres of reclaimed land just a couple of kilometres from the city centre, this huge resort complex includes a 27-hole golf course, swimming pools, a marina, a Golf and Country Club, spa and two 5-star hotels, offering a total of 17 restaurants and bars. The hotels are known as Magellan Sutera and Pacific Sutera, the latter often preferred by businessmen while holiday-makers often opt for the spacious, slightly more expensive Magellan.

ACCOMMODATION: WITHIN KOTA KINABALU

EXPENSIVE

Gayana Eco Resort
Ground floor, Wisma Sabah
Jalan Haji Saman
tel (088) 264461 / *fax* (088) 264460
info@gayana-eco-resort.com
www.gayana-eco-resort.com

Located in Malohom Bay on the edge of the Tunku Abdul Rahman Park in a bay on the northeast side of Pulau Gaya, this newly renovated, luxurious resort offers chalets over the water, with an attractively located restaurant at the end of a jetty. The resort also maintains a Marine Ecology Research Centre.

MODERATE

The Promenade
tel (088) 265555 / *fax* (088) 246666
enquiry@promenade.com.my
www.promenade.com.my

A 4-star hotel facing Gaya Bay and conveniently close to major shopping areas, this busy hotel especially favoured by visitors from Peninsular Malaysia also offers a gym and swimming pool.

Beverly Hotel
tel (088) 258998 / *fax* (088) 258778
reservation.bhkk@vhmis.com

Conveniently located 4-star hotel with pool and sea views from the 200 rooms and suites.

The Jesselton
tel (088) 223333 / *fax* (088) 240401
jesshtl@po.jaring.my
www.jesseltonhotel.com

Located in the heart of the business district, this charmingly restored small boutique hotel dates from 1954, and offers a unique ambience and excellent service plus a very popular restaurant and coffee shop.

Casuarina Hotel
tel (088) 221000 / *fax* (088) 243899

A small hotel tucked in a quiet lane within 5 minutes' walk of Tg Aru beach, this is popular with families. Friendly service. Free shuttle service to town; about 8 minutes from both the airport and the city.

BUDGET

Kinabalu Backpackers Lodge
4 Lorong Dewan
tel (088) 253 385
www.kinabalubackpackers.com

Located in the heart of old KK and within walking distance of just about everything, this small lodge offers free breakfast, dormitory rooms plus double and twin rooms. Laundry service, TV and DVD movies, free internet, storage and much more. Airport pickup can be arranged a day in advance.

Pulau Gaya/Tunku Abdul Rahman Park
Sutera Sanctuary Lodges
Ground floor, Lot 15, Wisma Sabah
Jalan Haji Saman, Kota Kinabalu
tel (088) 243629 / *fax* (088) 259552
info@suterasanctuarylodges.com

This company handles all reservations for Sabah Parks' chalets on Pulau Manukan, and also all accommodation within Kinabalu Park.

ACCOMMODATION: BEYOND KOTA KINABALU

KARAMBUNAI

Nexus Karambunai Resort
Karambunai, Off Jalan Sepangar
tel (088) 411222 / *fax* (088) 411020
info@nexusresort.com
http://www.nexusresort.com

This 5-star resort located on a long sandy beach offers just about every diversion one could wish, with golf, sea and river watersports, tennis, swimming pools, a gym and a relaxing spa, together with magnificent gardens and a range of restaurants. As they say in their advertisements, "some say it's heaven".

KINARUT

Langkah Syabas
Km 3.5 Jalan Papar Baru, Kg Laut Kinarut
tel (088) 752000 / *fax* (088) 752111
info@langkahsyabas.com.my
www.langkahsyabas.com.my

An attractive small resort with a swimming pool known for its good Western food and selection of wine, Langkah Syabas also runs a catamaran cruiser (*Fat Cat*) for fishing trips or visits to Dinawan Island.

Seaside Travellers Inn
Km 20 Jalan Papar, Kg Laut Kinarut
tel (088) 750555 / *fax* (088) 750479
stinnjo@tm.net.my
www.seasidetravellersinn.com.my

This family run hotel, with only 23 rooms, is popular for its seaside location and particularly warm, friendly service. Food can be enjoyed under the coconut palms or on the 1st floor balcony right at the water's edge; small pool, tennis and badminton courts, and sea kayaks for hire.

Klias Peninsula Garama River Lodge Only in Borneo Sdn. Bhd.
2nd floor, Lot 227–229 Wisma Sabah
Jalan Tun Fuad Stephens
tel (088) 260501 / *fax* (088) 261503
riverbug@traversetours.com
www.traversetours.com

Although most visitors opt for a day-trip to view proboscis monkeys, fireflies and other wildlife in the swamp, attractive chalet accommodation and 2 small dormitories are available for overnight stays.

Weston Wetland Paradise
Lot 12, 3rd floor, Block B, Damai
Plaza, Jalan Damai
tel (088) 239476, (019) 8218038
fax (088) 242809
tayweelet@westonwetland.com
www.westonwetland.com

Dormitory accommodation is currently being replaced by individual chalets. The dining lodge is built right on the water's edge. Wildlife viewing, crab catching, boat rides and wetland forest are the main attractions of this lodge near Weston, on the Klias Peninsula, 2 hours south of Kota Kinabalu. Comfortable rooms and chalets.

PULAU TIGA

Pulau Tiga Resort
Sipadan Dive Centre
A10-04 Wisma Merdeka, Phase 1,
Jalan Tun Razak
tel (088) 240584 / *fax* (088) 240415;
rsvn@pulautiga.com.my
www. pulautiga.com.my

The resort offers comfortable accommodation in chalets close to the beach, a variety of games and an airconditioned video room, scuba diving and a range of other sea sports. Plenty of opportunity for viewing birds, monitor lizards and monkeys, hiking trails and a mud bath beside a "mud volcano". Comfortable rooms and chalets.

ACCOMMODATION: BEYOND KOTA KINABALU

Shangri-La's Rasa Ria Resort
Pantai Dalit, Tuaran
tel (088) 792888 / *fax* (088) 792777
resv_rrr@shangri-la.com

A luxurious 5-star resort on a lovely quiet beach about 35 minutes from Kota Kinabalu, this offers a wide range of activities including water sports, golf, horse riding and a luxurious spa, together with a unique nature reserve where orangutans and other local wildlife can be seen. Rasa Ria has consistently won awards for its outstanding and friendly service. The resort's modern seaside restaurant, Coast, attracts visitors from Kota Kinabalu as well as hotel guests. A shuttle bus service runs 3 times daily to connect with their Tanjung Aru Resort in Kota Kinabalu.

Tuaran Beach Resort
Sabandar Beach, Tuaran
tel (088) 793593 / *fax* (088) 793594
info@tuaranbeachresort.com
www.tuaranbeachresort.com

This 4-star hotel, about 40 minutes from Kota Kinabalu, was taken over by new owners and renamed in 2007. A swimming pool, bicycle rental, a riding stable, children's playground and a 5-km beach ensure there are plenty of activities. Comfortable rooms and chalets.

SHOPPING

The major shopping complexes in Kota Kinabalu offer a wide range of products, from books to clothing, shoes, electronic equipment, computers, jewellery and souvenirs. There are also money changers, photo shops, hairdressers and tailors. While several large complexes are located in suburban areas, the following are the major ones in the city.

Centrepoint

The basement and lower floors of this large complex offer a wide range of shops, as well as a department store. The 4th and 5th floors, known as Palm Square, have a number of more exclusive boutiques selling well-known brands of clothing and shoes. There are also several food outlets on this floor, as well as food stalls in the basement.

Warisan Square

A number of major international and regional fashion brands, other boutiques, food franchises and a wide range of other stores are found in KK's newest downtown shopping mall, facing The Waterfront. There's a large Times bookshop on the ground floor and even a Thai spa.

Wisma Merdeka

The oldest air-conditioned shopping complex in town, this has two adjoining blocks where just about everything can be found. Some of the specialty stores here include a good range of books at Borneo Books (on the ground floor and second storey) and antique and curio stores on the second floor of the new block (known as Phase 2).

PHOTO CREDITS

The organizations or individual photographers listed below own all rights to the respective photographs used in this book as credited.

Michael Cadman
41 (left)

C.L. Chan
27, 40, 41 (right), 62

H.C. Chan
12–13, 34, 67, 74–76, 82, 85

C.V. Chong
i, ii, vi, 1, 7–11, 19, 22, 31–33, 38–39, 61, 64, 68, 78–81, 89

Wendy Hutton
14–17, 19 (top right), 20–26, 30, 35–37, 38, 42–43, 46–60, 63, 65, 70, 72–73, 77, 87

Lee Yen Phin
28–29

P.K. Lim
4

Jim Scott
44–45

Sabah Museum
3

experience
SABAH

Malaysian Borneo
www.sabahtourism.com

© Sabah Museum